In Front Of or Behind

Where's Eddie?

Daniel Nunn

Illustrations by Steve Walker

Raintree

Chicago, Illinois

Hide and Seek

www.capstonepub.com
Visit our website to find out
more information about
Heinemann-Raintree books.

To order:

☎ Phone 800-747-4992

💻 Visit www.capstonepub.com
to browse our catalog and order online.

Edited by Dan Nunn, Rebecca Rissman, and Sian Smith
Designed by Joanna Hinton-Malivoire
Picture research by Mica Brancic
Originated by Capstone Global Library, Ltd.
Production by Victoria Fitzgerald

Library of Congress Cataloging-in-Publication Data
Nunn, Daniel.
In front of or behind : where's Eddie? / Daniel Nunn.
p. cm.—(Hide and seek)
Includes bibliographical references and index.
ISBN 978-1-4109-4714-7 (hbk.)
ISBN 978-1-4109-4720-8 (pbk.)
1. Vocabulary—Juvenile literature. I. Title.
 PE1449.N774 2012
 428.1—dc23   2012000357

Acknowledgments
We would like to thank the following for permission to reproduce
photographs: Shutterstock pp.5 (© Losevsky Pavel), 6 (© Dmitry
Rukhlenko), 7 (© jomphong), 8 (© nito), 9 (© Tungphoto), 10 (©
Ihnatovich Maryia), 11, 12 (© vseb), 13, 14 (© WDG Photo), 15, 16
(© craftvision), 17, 18 (© Tomaz Kunst), 19, 20 (© Valentina R.), 21
(© Tihis), 22 (© Valentina R.), 23 (© Dudarev Mikhail).

Front cover photograph of cupcakes reproduced with permission
of Shutterstock (© Elena Talberg).

Every effort has been made to contact copyright holders of any
material reproduced in this book. Any omissions will be rectified in
subsequent printings if notice is given to the publisher.

Printed in the United States   5957

Contents

Be careful when you hide!
Eddie can hide in places where people can't. Hiding inside things can be very dangerous. Always ask an adult if it is safe first.

Meet Eddie the Elephant

This is Eddie the Elephant.

Eddie loves to play hide and seek!

Behind

Sometimes Eddie hides **behind** things.

When you are **behind** something,
that thing is **in front of** you.

Find Eddie!

Can you find Eddie?
Count to 10, then off you go!

Where is Eddie? Is he **in front of** the hippo or **behind** the hippo?

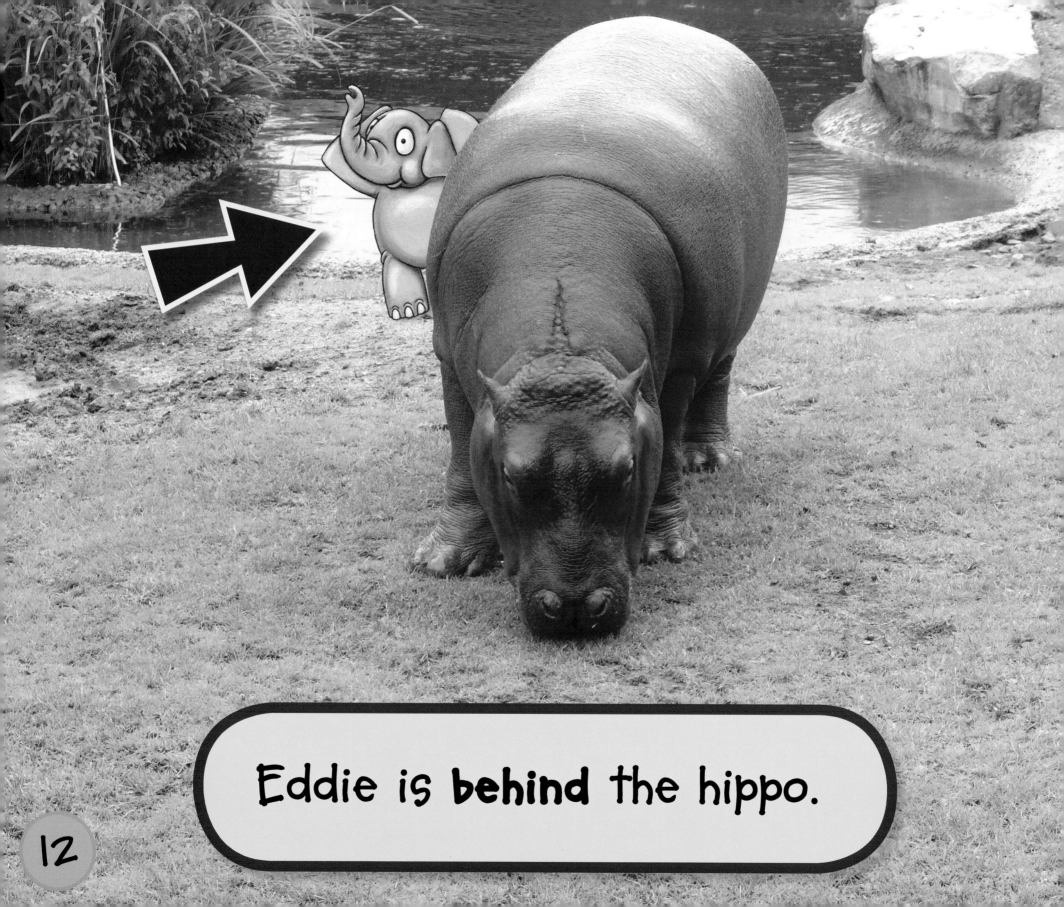

Eddie is **behind** the hippo.

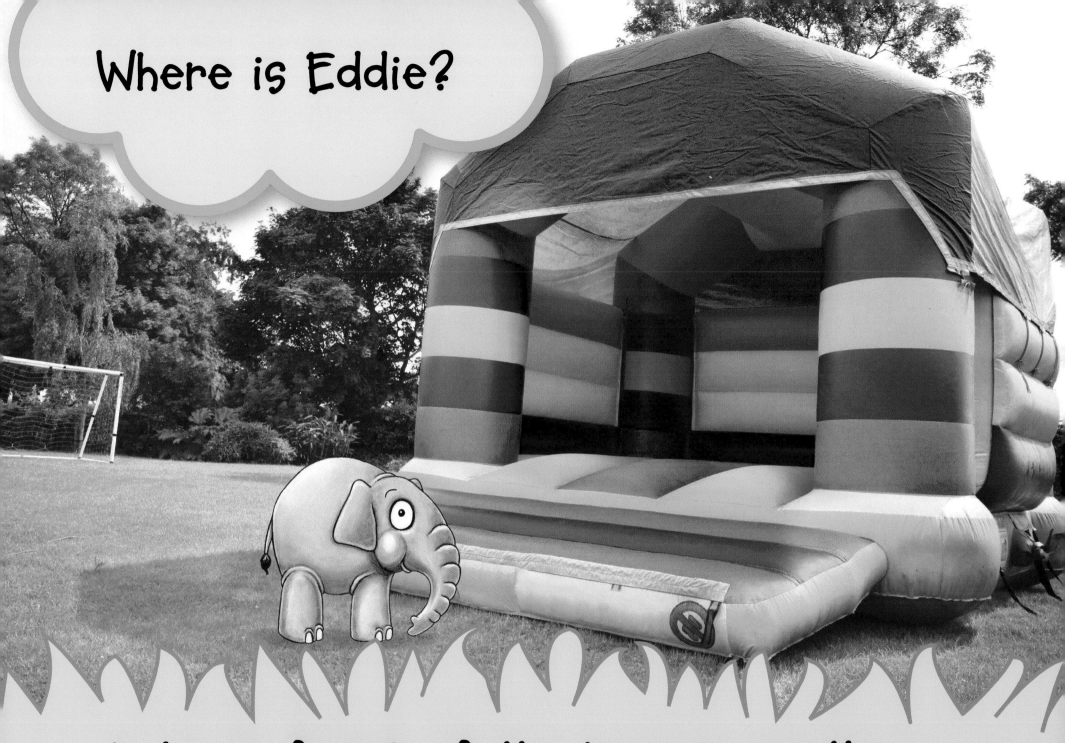

Is he **in front of** the bouncy castle or **behind** the bouncy castle?

Eddie is **in front of** the bouncy castle.

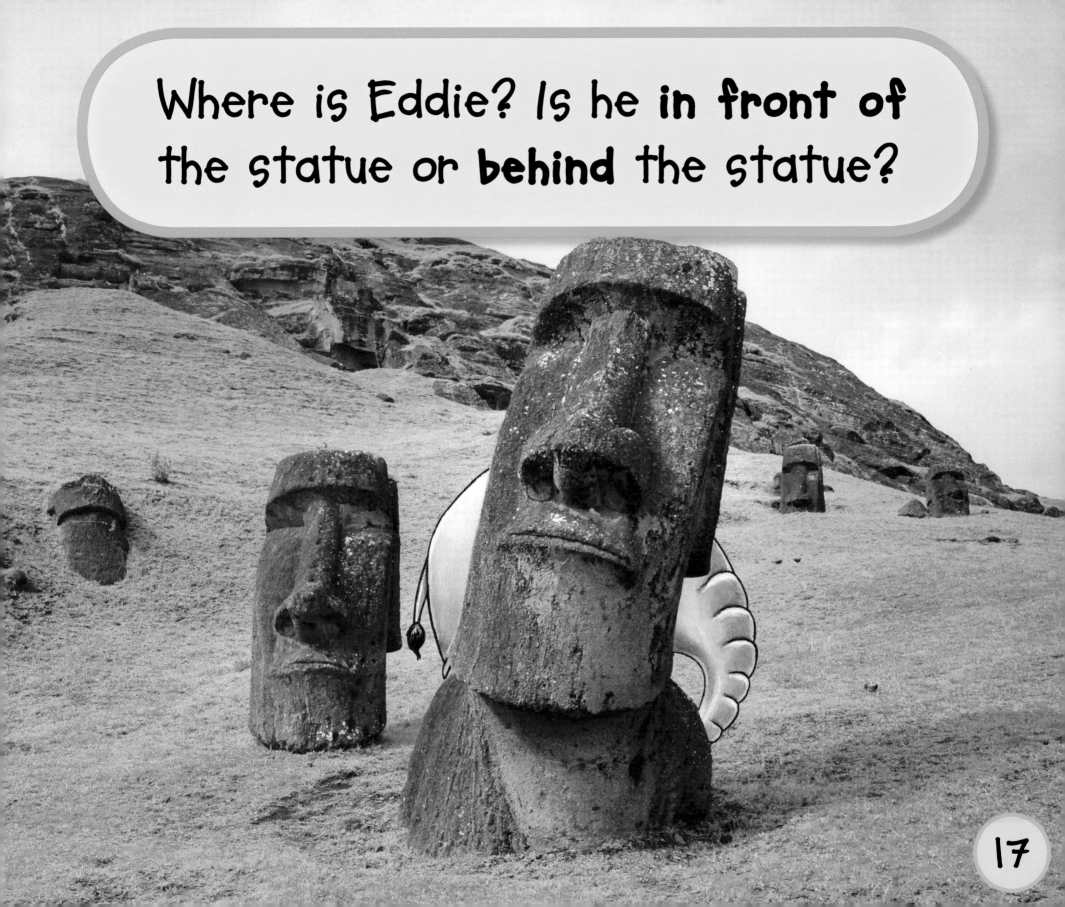

Where is Eddie? Is he **in front of** the apple or **behind** the apple?

19

Eddie is **behind** the apple.

True or False?

1. Eddie is **in front of** the snowman. True or false?

You can find the answers on page 24.

2. Eddie is **in front of** the teddy bear. True or false?

3. Eddie is **behind** the bicycle.
True or false?

Answers and More!

True or false?

1. True! Eddie is **in front of** the snowman.
2. False! Eddie is **behind** the teddy bear.
3. False! Eddie is **in front of** the bicycle.

Where can Eddie hide next?

Look around the room you are in.

What could Eddie hide **in front of**?

What could Eddie hide **behind**?